Herbert Feis, 1893 –

The Birth of
Israel

The Tousled Diplomatic Bed

W · W · NORTON & COMPANY · INC · NEW YORK

Contents

Foreword

THE TWENTY YEARS that have gone by since the birth of
the state of Israel have, in my opinion, clearly shown how
well justified was the desperate quest of the Jews for an
independent homeland; and how competently and cre-
atively they have striven to make it worthy. But the con-
flicts that attended its creation and scarred its birth have
not healed.

The antagonists, the Israelis and Arabs, still face primary decisions. For the Israelis the crucial political decision
may again be between a strong defense against attack or
cruel extinction. But the Israelis must also decide between
unyielding desire and a stance of restraint. They must not
allow their policy to be determined by military leaders and
should be satisfied with minimum advantages, if a peace
settlement is agreed to by the Arabs. For the Arabs the
choice is between the indefinite prolongation of hostility
and war, or acceptance of Israel on terms and within
boundaries that may be judged reasonable in the historical
circumstances. A new start must be made, burying the
past, improving the future.

The major powers have their own decisions to make regarding this deeply troubled and emotional situation. For

the United States, in the event of a serious danger that Israel may be destroyed, the choice lies between upholding her or suffering a bleeding historical ulcer which will not cease to hurt and poison. For the Soviet Union, the choice remains between cooperation with the West or cold expansive policy in the Arab world, which would increase the distrust of the rest of the world, and be a lasting denial of the ideals it professes.

History makes a great draught on our faith that the nations will manage to work out a peaceful, beneficial settlement for a mature Israel which comes of age in this year 1969.

This short study is, I know, not exhaustive, nor particularly original. But the tale is remarkable. The creation of Israel was, under the circumstances, an historical miracle. It was the one postwar international situation in which, at its climax, the United States and the Union of Soviet Socialist Republics were in accord; both sponsoring the birth, both eager to be recognized as well-wishing friends.

For help in providing the record of Israeli experience and in finding and checking sources of information, and for critical study of the manuscript, I am indebted to Giora Kulka, an Israeli, at present a graduate student in history at Harvard University. I am also grateful to Ambassador Loy Henderson, a former colleague in the State Department, for reminiscing with me about the tangles and twists in American policy in which he was so encoiled.

Herbert Feis

York, Maine
March, 1969

The Birth of Israel

1

"A National Home for the Jewish People"

ONE WISE TEACHER of the Zionists, reminiscing about the ordeal of the Jews in Palestine during the Second World War, wrote,

> . . . Once at least when Rommel stood at El Alamein it [the Jewish homeland] had passed through the valley of the shadow of death. There had been months when a frightful premonition of ultimate disaster had haunted us, and we had nightmares of the Germans and Italians marching into Palestine, and the cities and colonies, and tenderly nurtured achievements of two generations given over to the same destruction and pillage as German and Polish Jewry. It had not happened. . . . The war year . . . and the great war effort . . . had given the Jews of Palestine a heightened self-reliance.

The Jewish presence in Palestine had become by the end of the war so strong and tenacious that it could have been suppressed only by superior and ruthless force. But the Zionists' longing to develop into an independent national Jewish state was snagged by Arab opposition, and dependent on the decision of the great powers.

In the climax of creation of the state of Israel, the American Government stepped forward as foster parent. But it did so only after it had tried to evade direct responsibility.

The originators of political and diplomatic Zionism had first settled in the ancient land while it was still part of the former and tolerant Ottoman Empire. But by 1914 Jewish aspirations in Palestine had been doomed to wither under Turkish rule, grown oppressive of all national minorities. When Turkey joined Germany in the First World War, the British-oriented Zionist leaders got their chance of realizing their dream.

In November 1917, Arthur James Balfour, the Secretary of State for Foreign Affairs, had informed the Zionist leadership of what was "essentially a Cabinet decision." [1] It had been stated in a letter written by Balfour to Lord Rothschild:

> *I have much pleasure in conveying to you on behalf of His Majesty's Government the following declaration of sympathy with Jewish Zionist aspirations, which has been submitted to and approved by the Cabinet:*
>
> *His Majesty's Government view with favor the establishment in Palestine of a National Home for the Jewish people, and will use their best endeavour to facilitate the achievement of this object, it being clearly understood that nothing shall be done which*

> *may prejudice the civil and religious rights of exist-*
> *ing non-Jewish communities in Palestine. . . .*
>   *I should be grateful if you would bring this declar-*
> *ation to the knowledge of the Zionist Federation.*

The British Government had shown a draft of this Declaration to President Woodrow Wilson; he had approved
it; and that probably lessened the doubts and apprehen-
sions of the British sponsors. Wilson, wanting to make his
attitude known, had asked Secretary of the Navy Josephus
Daniels to do so at a large Zionist meeting.[2]

Ever since, there has been controversy over the intent
of the imprecise terms of the Declaration. What, at least,
Balfour had in mind is well established in the record; as
when, pressed rather unceremoniously by General Allenby's Chief Political Officer in Palestine, he said in a
small private gathering on February 7, 1918, "Both the
Prime Minister and myself have been influenced by a desire to give the Jews their rightful place in the world; a
great nation without a home is not right," and then added,
"My personal hope is that all the Jews will make good in
Palestine and eventually found a Jewish state." [3]

At the end of the First World War there had been, at
most, 50,000 Jews in Palestine. But under the Mandate
given in 1922 and British protection, immigration in-
creased and by 1928 the Jews, numbering 160,000, were
some 20 per cent of the total population (with 70 per cent
Moslems and 10 per cent Christians).[4] At least two-thirds
of the immigration during this period was from Russia and
Poland. But thereafter, the source changed, and the inflow
greatly rose. Soviet Russia refused to allow the Jews to
emigrate; the Polish Jews, scratched, even in their poor

villages, by Polish hostility and restrictions, continued to
come; and, as Hitler began to scourge the Jews, many
thousands set out for Palestine. Included in the new migration were not only farmers and laborers, but professional men and women, and small capitalists. After 1936,
because of active Arab opposition, the British Government
had set a maximum annual quota of less than 10,000 new-
comers. Then in 1939 in the White Paper, which was to
become for many the bar to survival, the limit of permis-
sible immigration during the next five years was set at
75,000. Illegal immigration had surged even before the
war, as in 1938–1939 the Jews were fleeing from Germany
and Austria to escape the Nazi scourge. Most could not
find another home, and many had become like lost souls,
wanderers over the seven seas, even Shanghai being for
a time a mass Jewish haven. But then the illegal immigration bureau set up by the Jewish Agency in Palestine had
chartered and manned ships, and by the time the war began eighteen shiploads of immigrants had been secretly
brought into Palestine.

During the Second World War Britain had used Palestine as a center of her armed forces and a source of supply
for its troops, until, after El Alamein, that center had
shifted to Egypt and North Africa. The Palestine Jews,
with grim alacrity, had made common cause with Britain
against Hitler. In August 1939 Chaim Weizmann, then
head of the Jewish Agency for Palestine, had offered the
Prime Minister, Neville Chamberlain, Palestinian Jewish
soldiers, resources, and professional help. Many thousands
of Jewish men and women had volunteered. The British
Middle East command had cooperated with the Jewish
Armed Forces. They had stood ready to defend Palestine
against the Axis; they had fought in Syria and engaged in

underground operations in the Balkans and Central Europe. As a Brigade group in the British Army they had fought well in Italy, East Africa, and North Africa. Deep in the hearts of these soldiers was the hope that their valor would validate their wish to form a Jewish home in Palestine, where Jews everywhere would be allowed freely to join them.

What support could the Palestine Jews expect from the United States at this time? The State Department, under Cordell Hull, had maintained the same stand as had Secretary of State Hughes nearly twenty years earlier: that the observance of the provision in the Balfour Declaration —that the Jews should be able to found a national center, "a home" in Palestine—and of the corresponding provision in the Mandate held by Britain, was not of primary or direct concern to the United States. President Franklin D. Roosevelt and the State Department alike were on guard lest by act or utterance they lend credence to German propaganda that the war had been brought about by Jews and Communists.

In March 1944 the Senate Committee on Foreign Relations considered a resolution that the American Government should use its good offices to secure the free entry of Jews into Palestine so that they might ultimately establish there an independent Jewish state. But Secretary of War Henry L. Stimson—that just man who at heart condemned Hitler's persecution most deeply—asked the Committee to suspend its consideration of this resolution. He was unwilling to risk a disturbance in the Middle East just before the invasion of Normandy was to get under way; he feared the possible need to divert British or American troops and ships in that event.[5]

During the election campaign of 1944, both American political parties had come out in favor of opening Palestine to unrestricted immigration and expressed support for the creation of a free and democratic Jewish commonwealth.[6] But again Congress was persuaded not to go forward with a public resolution.

Roosevelt had not spoken out personally in support of the Zionist program. But he had authorized Rabbi Stephen Wise to tell newsmen that he gave his full backing to the Palestine plank in the Democratic platform.[7] And he had sent a message to the Annual Conference of the Zionist Organization which was to be read by Senator Robert F. Wagner of New York. In this Roosevelt promised, "If elected I shall help to bring about its [the Democratic platform plank on Palestine] realization." [8]

But the election over, and Arab opposition becoming vocal, he hurried off from the Yalta Conference in February 1945 to meet Ibn Saud, ruler of Saudi Arabia, and told him that no decision of consequence about Palestine would be made before discussion with both Arabs and Jews. He confirmed this promise in a letter a week before his death.

Roosevelt's caution may have been fostered by the extension of American activities and interests in the region as the war went on; the Air Force and Navy wanted to acquire permanent bases in the region; and the eyes of the American oil executives had grown large as they studied the geological reports of the vast underground oil resources in the Arab lands. Still—and beyond these strong reins of national interest—there is reason to believe that Roosevelt cherished the illusion that presumably he, and he alone, as head of the United States, could bring about a settlement—if not a reconciliation—between Arabs and Jews. I remember muttering to myself as I left the White House after hearing the President discourse in rambling fashion about Middle Eastern affairs, "I've read of men who thought they might be King of the Jews and other men who thought they might be King of the Arabs, but this is the first time I've listened to a man who dreamt of being King of both the Jews and Arabs."

The British authorities had taken great risks and made great exertions to retain their influence in the Arab countries. They regarded Britain's relations with Egypt as crucial because of the Suez Canal; moreover, Egypt and Iraq had provided very large quantities of goods and services during the war for which payment was due and frozen. They looked to this Middle Eastern region as the only large satisfactory supplier of oil for Britain, since it could be bought there for sterling. And looming over the situation was uncertainty about India's future and—settling deeply in Churchill's mind—fear of Russian attempts to extend their realm in all directions. Thus Churchill, though a supporter of Zionism, maintained that the time had not yet come for a Jewish state.

The specter of violent Arab opposition to any move toward creation of a Jewish state in Palestine had appeared in March 1945, when the governments of Egypt, Syria, Lebanon and Saudi Arabia signed a pledge to take united action to protect the Arab position in Palestine and Trans-Jordan.

So shimmering, then, was the Middle Eastern scene, so touched by streaks of lightning was the project of creating a Jewish state in Palestine, when in April 1945 Harry S. Truman became President of the United States, and when in July 1945 the Conservative British Government yielded to the Labour Government.

2

⋘⋘⋘⋘⋘⋘⋘⋘⋘⋘

The British-American Effort

OF THE TWO new Administrations, the British Labour Government seemed more settled on a Palestine policy than the American.

At eleven annual Labour Party conferences, resolutions had been voted in support of Zionist aims. In the one passed in December 1944, it had been declared that "There is surely neither hope nor meaning in a Jewish National Home unless we are prepared to let Jewry . . . enter this tiny land in such numbers as to become a majority . . ." As recently as May 1945—a few weeks before the general election—the Labour Party had reaffirmed that it was " . . . in favor of building Palestine as the Jewish National Home." Almost all its leaders in Parliamentary debates or campaign speeches had expressed personal favor for that cause. The Prime Minister, Clement Attlee, and Secretary for Foreign Affairs, Ernest Bevin, having been in the War Cabinet, were conversant with the Arab problem and these resolutions.

Hardly had President Truman seated himself at his desk

when Secretary of State Edward Stettinius counseled him to be reserved toward the Zionist demand for unrestricted immigration into Palestine. Shortly thereafter, Stettinius having left for the United Nations Conference in San Francisco, Acting Secretary of State Joseph Grew sent the new President a reminder of the promise which Roosevelt had made to Ibn Saud. The State Department was receiving vehement letters of protest from the Arab leaders. Nokrashy Pasha, Egypt's Premier, wrote directly to Truman asking why Palestine, a small nation of one million people living in a very small territory, should be forced to accept within twenty-five years immigrants of an alien race up to nearly 50 per cent of their own number.

The answer which history was to give sprang from the concentration camps and displaced-persons assembly points in Central Europe. The flow of Jewish refugees and migrants turned to Palestine because once there they might be able to live, no longer frightened and miserable outcasts, but determined and respected creators of a home of their own. It was fended toward that country by the refusal of the United States and other countries to admit more than a small number of those who needed succor, or desperately wanted out.[1]

Only when American troop carriers entered the concentration camps, followed by press correspondents, did most Americans realize the full gruesome horror of what had been done to the Jews of Central and Eastern Europe, and the miserable plight and deep shock of the survivors. Many new ardent supporters in the United States and elsewhere, some with substantial means, began to espouse the Zionist cause. The aim of providing a permanent place of refuge, a haven for the survivors in Europe and the Jews scattered throughout the Moslem world, was being transformed from the wishful dream of a few into a broadly international political cause. The suffering of the Jews touched even distant and comfortable hearts, over-riding prejudice.

President Truman was similarly moved and convinced. But the focusing on Palestine of the search for a refuge compelled him to reckon—as he would feel compelled to do during the whole crisis of the creation of Israel—with the risks involved in aiding the Zionist cause. How simple to be an ardent advocate, and how easy to be a generous contributor to a cause! How much harder to be the just and beneficent decision-maker placed in a tensile, electric field of circumstance and national interest. What would be the effect on American relations with Britain, the mandatory power, and on those with the Soviet Union, whose tentacles had long hovered over the region? How might American interest in the oil of the Arab Middle East and our presumptive strategic position be affected? How would American opinion react in the face of foreign and domestic opposition?

Beset by such considerations, Truman discussed the problems of Palestine with Churchill when in July 1945 they met at the Potsdam Conference. They had in common the determination to resist current Russian efforts to force entry into Iran, to gain control of the Straits of the Dardanelles, and to obtain a base in the Eastern Mediterranean.

On July 24 Truman wrote to Churchill, pointing out the great interest Americans had in Palestine and their wish that the restrictions on Jewish immigration into that land maintained by Britain be lifted "without delay." Had Churchill remained in power, it is probable that he would have agreed at least to the plea of the Jewish Agency to grant 100,000 more permits for Jewish immigrants to Palestine. But before the great wartime Conservative Prime Minister could reply, he was ejected from office.

The provisional answer given on July 31 by Clement Attlee, his successor, was noncommittal. Gusts of indignant doubt began to mar the rejoicing of the Zionists over the advent of the Labour Party—which had so steadfastly endorsed Zionism. Attlee and Bevin, the new Secretary for Foreign Affairs, harkened to the advice of permanent officials in the Foreign Office and the Colonial Office who dealt with the affairs of Palestine, particularly the senior adviser, Harold Beeley. They were more sympathetic to Arab plaints than to Jewish pleas. Diplomacy should be directed, they thought, toward the maintenance, with combined British and American support, of an Arab fence to prevent Russian entry into the area. The Mandatory Administration could look forward to prolonged tenure of rule over the Palestine Arabs, but were afraid of the unruly Jews. Thus the answer of the Colonial Office to the Jewish Agency was that no more than 1,500 immigration certificates a month would be issued.[2] Attlee and Bevin stood by this answer, and they stood fast against American recommendations that the restrictions on Jewish migration and settlement in Palestine be relaxed to permit admission of a much greater number of survivors of Nazi persecution.

But Truman would not desist, and the clamor of the Zionists and their supporters throughout the world grew louder and angrier. What, they asked, of the former pledges of the Labour Party? What of the traditional British sympathy with the suffering? The defensive explanation given was that Britain was not indifferent to the plight of the Jews; to the contrary, it wished to salvage them and enable them to start life anew. But why, in face of Arab objections and the challenged British position in the Middle East, must they be permitted to crowd into Palestine? And should they be, would the American Government provide forces and finances if the Arab nations—possibly with Russian aid—were to resist by arms?

By this time the anger of the Jews in Palestine against British restraints was becoming strong and active. The Haganah (Hebrew for *defense*), the illegal Jewish armed force which had been formed to defend Jewish settlements against attacking Arab bands, had opposed the terrorists, until it became plain that the British Labour Government was going to resist—and possibly defeat—the Zionist cause. Then, despite Weizmann's vehement objections, most of the leadership of the Palestine Jews came to regard the methods of the terrorist elements as the only way to weaken British control. The underground units began to destroy radar installations, police stations, railways, and bridges. The Haganah sometimes shielded and helped the terrorist groups, sometimes suppressed them.

The Haganah also strove desperately to arrange a movement of Jewish immigration into Palestine far greater than the British authorities would permit.[3] Despite appeals and supplications by the Jewish Agency, the British Government had maintained its restrictions during the war against the tide of Jewish refugees flowing from Central Europe along the Danube River to Black Sea ports. The Zionist organization continued to send them along illegally; some found their way into Palestine, others were torpedoed, or sent to the African island of Mauritius, or, having been stranded in a decrepit ship (the *Struma*) in the port of Istanbul, were towed out to sea, where the ship exploded and all but one of the 769 refugees on board drowned.[4]

In 1945, when the Second World War ended, there were in Palestine about 600,000 Jews and about twice that number of Arabs. While most of the Jews lived in urban centers, the Arabs were preponderantly in rural districts—farmers, shepherds, nomads.[5]

Attlee sought to lighten the pressure on Britain, and to have the United States match advice with obligation. So he proposed to Truman on October 19 that an Anglo-American Committee of Inquiry be formed. Let it, he suggested, consider all possible lanes of relief for the harmed and forsaken Jews of Europe, not merely Palestine; resettlement in their countries of origin or of present residence, migration to all other regions. Let us wait, he urged, until this Committee recommends measures to deal with the emergency, pending a more permanent solution through the United Nations. While the Committee was pursuing its inquiries, the existing rules regarding Jews' entry into and settlement in Palestine were to be retained.

Truman responded to the proposal that a qualified Committee—half English, half American—look into and over the whole distressing and distracting dilemma. But, he told Attlee, he thought the Committee's inquiries should be focused toward the possibilities of Palestine. The President, it may be surmised, wanted to eliminate the

chance that the demand for admission of immigrants
be turned toward the United States. Moreover, he em-
phasized in his response to Attlee his wish that the Committee do its job speedily.

When Attlee visited Washington in November 1945, in
search for assurance that the American Government would
share knowledge of production of atomic weapons with
Britain—as Roosevelt was thought to have promised
Churchill—he and Truman reached an accord on the nature of this Committee and its assignment. The two governments concurrently issued on November 13 statements
of their respective and divergent positions. Bevin, regret-
tably, at this time allowed his exasperation at the persis-
tence of the Jews to burst out publicly in expressions
which intensified their sense that he had turned against
them. At a press conference he remarked that "If Jews,
with all their suffering, want to get too much at the head
of the queue, you have the danger of another anti-Semitic
reaction to it all." [6] There spoke all his suppressed irrita-
tion at the nagging, past and present, of the Zionists, and
the weight of the gloomy warnings which Foreign and
Colonial Office advisers laid on.

Even before the Committee of Inquiry set about its
assignment, the American Congress showed its unconcern
over the imperial worries that were making Attlee and
Bevin distraught. On December 19 it passed a resolution
enjoining the American Government to secure "free entry
of Jews into Palestine so that they might have a chance to
proceed to erect a Jewish National Home." Three days
later the President issued a statement advocating more
expeditious procedures for regulating the immigration of
refugees into the United States. But he did not urge or
recommend changes in American restrictive legislation.
Thus the statement had little actual consequence.

Just then, Secretaries James Byrnes (who had succeeded Stettinius five months before) and Bevin were in Moscow at a meeting of the Council of Foreign Ministers. There they were seeking to bridge grave differences with the Soviet Government over the procedure for arriving at peace treaties with Italy and Hitler's European satellites. And they were trying to get the Soviet Union to withdraw its troops from Iran, where they were assisting subversive and secessionist elements. Truman, at this juncture, was still not so aroused by Russian threats, or so disturbed by the pending dissolution of the British Empire, as to smother his feeling about Palestine. But the British authorities were; and so were some State Department officials, concerned with global policy. As flatly summed up by Loy Henderson, Chief of the Near East Division of the State Department, in talking with Bartley Crum, one of the American members of the Committee of Inquiry, "There is one fact facing the United States and Great Britain. That is the Soviet Union. It would be wise to bear that in mind when you consider the Palestine problem." [7]

The personnel of the Committee were announced in December—six Americans, six Englishmen—all men of repute but of diverse temperament and connection, headed by two judges, one American, one British.[8] The Committee began its work by holding hearings in Washington, then in London. While the Committee was in London, at a luncheon given in its honor, Bevin impulsively said he would implement any report that was unanimous. Thereafter the Committee dispersed over Western Europe, to meet again as a group in Cairo and to travel on separate itineraries through Palestine.

The visions and sympathies of the American and British members diverged, but not as greatly nor as inflexibly as might have been expected. Each, as a result of his travels and interviews, got his own impressions and formed his own opinions. To two or three of the more sensitive, the sight of the human cinders that were found at the doors of the gas chambers was a traumatic experience. None could have been left unaware that the Jews in the refugee camps in Germany and Austria would never of their own free will return to those countries, that the only faith that had not been burnt out of them was that of starting again in the Jewish homeland. As remembered by Richard Crossman, one of the British group, "A pathetic but obstinate determination to survive made them assert that each day in Germany must be lived as though it was the last day, when food is eaten hurriedly, when bags are packed ready for the journey out of the land of Egypt and into the Promised Land." [9]

Almost all of the British group continued to feel that to admit many thousands more Jews into Palestine would be unjust as well as offensive to the Arabs, and upsetting to their way of life. Still all members—English as well as Americans—at the end of their examination of the problem verged toward several main conclusions. They were:

That the idea of a National Home in Palestine was not a conception nurtured by wealthy foreign Jews but so deep a wish of many Jews of Western Europe, especially the refugees, that they would give their lives for it;

That these Jews would not, no matter what the compulsion, return to their countries of origin where they had suffered so greatly and where their relatives and their communities had been wiped out;

That there was little or no chance that foreign countries, including the United States, would accept any substantial number of them as immigrants;

That, therefore, Palestine should be opened to them.

These conclusions shaped the recommendations of the Committee, although it strove also to keep other solutions open and to moderate the opposition of the Arabs. The unanimous report recommended the immediate issuance of immigration certificates for 100,000 Jews (approximately the number then in the refugee camps of Germany and Austria). But it observed that Palestine was not a sufficiently large country to be a haven for all the Jews who wanted to emigrate. The Committee therefore stated that other countries should provide homes for them.

The proponents of partition on the Committee bowed to the majority who believed that any attempt to establish separate states would result in civil war. Therefore, it was recommended that Palestine should remain unified under the existing Mandate until a trusteeship agreement under the United Nations was reached. Within the country there should not be a separate Jewish nor an Arab state; neither should dominate the other. In the interim period the administration of Palestine should continue to facilitate Jewish immigration to the extent that conditions permitted—a vague formula; and the existing restrictions on the sale, lease, or use of land in Palestine to the Jews should be rescinded.

These recommendations, contained in the report of the Anglo-American Committee of April 20, 1946, were welcomed in Washington and rebuffed in London.

Truman, on making the report public on April 30, said he agreed with the substance of the proposals, and he urged that the recommendation for 100,000 entry certificates be heeded at once. "The transference of these unfortunate people," he remarked, "should now be accomplished with the greatest dispatch."

The British Government was greatly upset. All its traditional and valued connections with the Arab world were being contorted. A treaty granting independence to Trans-Jordan had been negotiated; but King Abdullah was being bitterly criticized by his Arab neighbors for allowing Britain to continue to station its troops in his country. Another treaty was being negotiated with Egypt but its reception was in doubt (later the treaty offer was rejected for the ostensible reason that the British would not go back on their pledge to the Sudanese that they would be permitted to determine their own political future).[10] Now Britain was being pushed to accept a plan for Palestine which, it was foreseen, would arouse the Arabs without placating the Jews. So does history tug all the harder at weakening cords of power.

Bevin was in a black rage because Truman had chosen to pluck one recommendation out of the report and feature it. Prime Minister Attlee, restrained as usual, told the House of Commons on May 1 that the report should be considered "as a whole with all its implications." Even if this were done, he continued, the British Government would not take on itself, alone, the risk and strain and expense of carrying out the Committee's recommendations. It would therefore seek to ascertain what share the United States would bear of the additional military and financial liabilities that would have to be incurred.

In any case, Attlee concluded, Britain would not permit large-scale Jewish immigration unless the Zionists disbanded their underground armed forces and ended their terrorism. For, anguished by the heartless way in which old vessels carrying desperate, stricken refugees to the Promised Land were being turned away from the shores of Palestine, the Palestinian Jews were striking back with cruelty and ferocity.[11]

Truman, advised by Under Secretary of State Dean Acheson, paid deference to the vehemence of British objections. Why should not both governments, he asked Attlee on May 8th, initiate talks with the Arabs and the Jews in regard to the recommendation that 100,000 Jews be admitted into Palestine without delay. Perhaps he thought these consultations would be a formality, in conformity with the promise Roosevelt had given Ibn Saud. Or perhaps he thought the Arabs might be persuaded to accede to this as an emergency measure. Or that the British might find these talks useful in calming the Zionists. Attlee was willing to engage in these talks; but in no hurry.

Meanwhile the Arab diplomats in Washington, in formal regalia, called on Acheson and Henderson to scorch the American Government with the heat of their opposition. They wanted national independence for Palestine as a whole, and Arab rule therein would be jeopardized by further Jewish immigration and the establishment of a separate Jewish authority within Palestine.

Truman sought the opinion of the Joint Chiefs of Staff. They warned against involving American armed forces in carrying out the Committee's recommendations, against any step that would so inflame the situation in Palestine that the British troops might alone be incapable of controlling it. For the United States should not endanger Western oil interests in the Middle East, nor cause the Arabs to open their arms to Russia. In sum, the Joint

Chiefs advised, let the British decide the course and bear the consequences—as if the United States could really remain on the side lines.

Truman, mindful of these admonitions, began to tread water. Bevin's anger was not subsiding. He let it be known that he thought that Truman's statement approving the report had been dictated by domestic politics and activated by large Jewish contributions to the Democratic Party. Speaking at a Labour Party Conference on June 1, he blurted out that the reason why Truman was pressing to have the Jews admitted to Palestine was because Americans did not want any more Jews in New York City.[12] This was in effect an insinuation that the Americans, not he, were the anti-Semites.

By this time, it should be borne in mind, both the British and American Governments were angry and upset at Russia's efforts to extend its reach and power in the Eastern Mediterranean and toward the Persian Gulf; it had asked Turkey to cede two northern provinces and had sought the right to garrison the Straits of the Dardanelles; it had plotted to set up a puppet government in Iranian Azerbaijan and demanded oil concessions; it was striving to obtain control over one of the former Italian colonies in North Africa.

But their common opposition to these Russian moves did not draw the Americans and British closer together in regard to Palestine. So nasty in its outspokenness did the difference of views become that had it been allowed to run free and further it might have prevented the concert of American and British policies in European affairs. So Truman, in response to Attlee's pleas, agreed to review the problem again with the British. For that purpose he asked a Cabinet committee to appoint members of another group which was to meet with their counterparts in London. He sent them over on June 10 for two weeks of consultation. Neither its American Chairman, Henry Grady, former Assistant Secretary of State, nor its English Chairman, Lord Morrison, nor any of its other members, were qualified by knowledge either of Zionism or of Palestine, or deeply concerned over the plight of the Jews. They were rather indifferent officials.

This second Anglo-American group, predictably, submitted on July 10 recommendations at variance with those of its predecessor. Ignoring the intensity of the struggle within Palestine, they suggested the creation of a Federal State of the two provinces, one smaller Jewish province, and one larger Arab province. Immigration would be controlled by a central government—the Executive of which was to be appointed by the British Government. Since in one of the two contemplated legislative chambers the Arabs would have majority, they would, it could be inferred, be enabled to prevent or limit future Jewish immigration.

This arrangement provided no solution for the immediate problem of the Jewish refugees. It did not satisfy the Zionist determination to manage Jewish affairs without continued constraint of the hated British administration. Neither was it acceptable to the Arabs, since it contemplated a permanent and largely self-governing Jewish province.

The flight of Jews into Palestine was at its height when in early August 1946 the British Government announced that all captured "illegal" immigrants would be deported to the island of Cyprus, to be released at the rate of 1500 a month as fixed in the quota that had been set by Bevin in September 1945.[13] The British were shutting out refugees from war-destroyed villages and towns, survivors of

concentration-death camps and the gas chambers. With
every barbed-wire corral that British troops strung in
Cyprus, the world was reminded of nauseating parallels
with Hitler's concentration camps, and in all Western
lands indignation and criticism rose. But except for a few
Latin-American countries none opened their gates more
widely to offer a home for Jews other than Palestine.

Britain, left to cope with the problem, trying to crush
the immigration in order to prevent the Jews from becoming dominant in Palestine, lost the world's sympathy. Its
hard-hearted repulses of the immigrant ships that tried to
reach Israel smirched its name, and began even to becloud
memory of its most valiant struggle against the Nazis. The
suffering of the desperate pilgrims evoked sympathy, and
the tales of the vicissitudes of individual ships were fea-
tured in the press, and became historical legends.[14]

In the United States the plan of the second Anglo-
American group was brusquely and generally criticized,
and on August 12 the Truman Administration rejected it.

Thus ended the effort of the two allies to reconcile their
views jointly to devise an arrangement whereby Jews and
Arabs could live together peacefully in Palestine. On this
they remained opposed to each other even while the
United States provided the means to revive Britain's economic vitality and relieve distress in the rest of western
Europe—through the Marshall Plan. The inclination to
save Hitler's victims was to sway American diplomacy,
despite the British effort to preserve its Empire, U.S. concern over oil, and mutual suspicion of Russian designs.
Perhaps, who knows—destiny works in curious ways and
history keeps its secrets—the refugee scientists who had
fled their countries, among them Albert Einstein, Enrico

Fermi, James Franck, and Leo Szilard, who did so much to produce the atomic bomb, were, unforeseeably, protecting those victims of Hitler who sought a new life in Israel, by enabling American diplomacy in the Middle East to be bolder during the critical time.

3

✦✦✦✦✦

The United Nations Resolves on Partition

IT WAS THE AUTUMN of 1946, and the American election campaign for Congress was under way. The Democrats and their opponents rivaled each other in their advocacy of admission of Jews into Palestine. On the eve of Yom Kippur (the Jewish Day of Atonement), October 4, President Truman again publicly advocated that a substantial number of Jews should be admitted into Palestine at once, without waiting for a basic solution. He offered to pay the expense of transporting them to that country and of aiding them to make the new land productive. Against Attlee's reprimand and Arab recriminations, the President stood his ground. At this time the British authorities were trying on their own, by separate and assiduous conferences in Paris and London with Arab and Zionist leaders, to find some mutually acceptable arrangement. They failed. Bevin was to allege later (in the House of Commons on February 25, 1947) that he might have succeeded in getting the Arabs and Jews to confer with each other had not Truman issued this statement. This was wishful thinking.[1] Bevin also recalled that he had pleaded with Secretary of State Byrnes to dissuade the President, but that Byrnes had said that if Truman did not speak out to this effect, his rival Dewey would.[2]

Aggrieved, worn down by domestic and foreign troubles, the British Government decided to cease trying to be arbiter of the murderous antagonists in Palestine. At this time Britain had 50,000 troops there, more than one-tenth of its army, as well as units of the Trans-Jordan Arab Legion and 10,000 British and local police. Despite the violent troubles in Palestine, the British Army authorities had continued to move war stores from Egypt to Palestine, with the thought that it could be a substitute base for Suez.

Since the United States would not help, let the United Nations—created to end disputes—try! Whether or not the British authorities reckoned that they would be besought to retain the Mandate, or whether they were really reconciled to giving it up—come what may—is unclear. Possibly Bevin hoped that Britain would retain it, since he asked the UN to decide how its Mandate "can be administered . . . or amended." Most British officials wanted, if possible, to retain the Mandate both for strategic reasons and as protection for oil supplies that could be paid for in sterling. But the fact was that during the awful winter months ahead, the British people could hardly have borne any greater outlay for Palestine. The Marshall Plan was not yet conceived. Bevin, at this last moment, offered still another plan under which immigration restrictions would have been slightly and temporarily relaxed. But the Zionists rejected it.

Thereupon on February 18th, Bevin, in the House of Commons, recapitulating British efforts to find a way of adjusting Jewish and Arab claims, said that the Government could do no more. Since it was not willing to incur any longer the cost and criticism, it had ". . . reached the conclusion that the only course now open to us is to submit the problem to the judgment of the United Nations." His Government, he added, would not recommend any particular solution. On this same date the Foreign Secretary said also, "I still want to make one further appeal to other countries in the world—to the United States of America and to everybody else—to help with these displaced persons." The appeal died out before it reached Capitol Hill.

When, on April 2, the British Government requested the Secretary General of the UN to put Palestine on the agenda of the next meeting of the Assembly, it said nothing of its further intentions.

The Zionists, by then suspicious of every British action, were puzzled by this one. They wondered whether Bevin was not just being cunning; whether he did not believe that a clash between the United States and the Soviet Union would prevent the General Assembly from agreeing on any resolution, and in this event that Britain would be asked to continue to administer the Mandate with refreshed authority. This might have happened had not, surprisingly, the American and Soviet Governments both opted for partition as the debate went on.

It was an unexpected alignment. During this same spring of 1947 President Truman had, in proposing aid for Greece and Turkey, announced a policy of frontal opposition to any and all further Communist attempts to subvert "free" nations—the Soviet Government being the unnamed but plainly indicated culprit.

The Assembly that opened on April 28, 1947, heard the

British representative, Sir Alexander Cadogan, state that his Government would no longer try to shape the form or future of Palestine. The American representative, Warren Austin, took up the lead, proposing that the Assembly create a Special Committtee on Palestine (which became known as UNSCOP) to seek a solution. This should, it was suggested, be authorized to negotiate, and asked to report to the next regular session of the Assembly in the autumn.

At this juncture the Soviet Government suddenly injected itself in the situation, with evident bias against the British stand. Ambassador Gromyko agreed to the American proposal. But he urged insistently that the five permanent members of the Security Council should be the nucleus of this special committee. Presumably each of these would have a veto power as in the Security Council. Austin objected. The real reasons for his opposition may be safely conjectured: that he believed there was little chance of agreement in a group within which the United States, the USSR, and Britain confronted one another at close range; and that the American Government did not want to have the Soviet Union included in the discussion for fear that it would thereby claim the right to participate in the future direction of the affairs of Palestine. Soviet intentions, the American authorities had by then inferred, were sinister; Russia's purpose, it was thought, would be not to quiet trouble, but to excite it.

The issue was avoided by an agreement that none of the great powers would be represented on the special commission; UNSCOP's eleven members would be appointed by the governments of Australia, Canada, Czechoslovakia, Guatemala, India, Iran, the Netherlands, Peru, Sweden, Uruguay, and Yugoslavia. Students of this list

could draw many inferences regarding the probable course
of its discussions and nature of its recommendations. But
none could or did foresee that the individual representing
the smallest country, Guatemala, would play a leading
role both in the Committee's discussions and in the Assembly's reception of the Committee's report. Jorge Garcia-
Granados was the Guatemalan Ambassador in Washington. He was militantly opposed to British policy in
Palestine. During UNSCOP's visit in Palestine he untiringly maintained that the UN authority must not be
hindered by the British administration; and he was open
in his opposition to British restrictive regulations. In the
discussions within UNSCOP he was usually supported by
the Uruguayan and Yugoslav representatives.[3]

Few anticipated, until Gromyko spoke out on May
14 in the Assembly, that the Soviet Government would
definitely favor the Jewish aspiration for a national home.
Emigré Jews from Russia had been the torchbearers of
the Zionist movement. But the Czarist authorities had
ignored them, and although Jews had been prominent
in the revolutionary and early Communist Government,
Stalin was anti-Semitic and acidly anti-Zionist, morbidly
seeing the hand of Jews in activities he disliked, and
hateful toward the few he knew, among them his son-in-
law and daughter-in-law.[4] Why the Soviet authorities
took up their course can only be inferred from the record
of their past and current diplomacy, looking toward, always looking toward, the Persian Gulf and the Mediterranean. There can be little doubt that Gromyko was
scheming in that direction when he said to the Assembly
on this day that the ideal situation would be a dual Arab-
Jewish state, but since that could not be wrought, the
Soviet Government would support partition and the creation of two independent states.

A covey of conjectures crowd the mind when it seeks to reason why the Soviet Union—even its revolutionary Communist regime—while refusing to permit Jews in Russia to emigrate, exercised its influence in behalf of the creation of a Jewish state. Was it in the hope of causing a crack in the solidifying U.S.-British structure of cooperation that was forming? Was it foresight that even partition would not bring peace to the Middle East, that the Arabs would long continue to rage against the allocation of a part of Palestine as an independent Jewish state, and sooner or later would invite or enable the Soviet Union to acquire the influence Great Britain would lose? Or was it with the hope that if the plan ultimately developed, the Soviet Union would have, through the United Nations, a share in the direction of developments in Palestine? Or was it because of awareness that most of the people in the satellite countries, and perhaps in Russia also, were anti-Semitic and would be glad if the Jews went to Palestine? Such queries must await study by later historians of official records now held secret.

The British authorities in Palestine had been detouring the uncertified Jewish immigrants to Cyprus. Then in the summer of 1947 their patience broke, and in their wrath they behaved most cruelly, so cruelly that their action long slashed their countenance. In July the largest consigment of immigrants to date—4500 of them—men, women, children, young and old, all wretched, set out from the port of Sète in Southern France for Palestine on the ship *European Exodus.* This was the name for the re-used, broken-down, old American river-boat, the *President Warfield,* no longer judged seaworthy by either the French or Italian Governments. The French authorities had refused to issue a certificate authorizing it to carry

passengers, but, despite Bevin's demand, had let it slip
out to sea.

The *Exodus* was not given the chance to make a dash
for the shores of Palestine. It was intercepted by British
destroyers twenty miles at sea. The British boarded it,
fought with the passengers, and announced that they
would be sent back to Europe. They carried this order
into effect despite the warning of the British High Commissioner in Palestine, who notified the Foreign Office that
this action would excite the Jews in Palestine to more
relentless terrorism.

The decrepit ship with its miserable passengers reached
a French harbor, and the French Government stated it
would allow any of the refugees who wished to stay in
France. Few did; they were bound for Palestine.

Thereupon the British Government ordered the ship to
sail for Germany, the land of their agony. At Hamburg all
were forced to disembark, and were interned in a camp
outside the city.

If the British Government had hoped by this severity to
assert its authority not only over the Zionists but also over
the UN Special Committee on Palestine, it failed. The
effort to do so alienated even friends in the United States
and France, and gave the Soviet Government the chance
to pose as the humane befriender of the Jews.[5]

UNSCOP reported to the Assembly in September that
all its members agreed that the Mandate should be ended
and that, under UN auspices, some form of independence
be granted to Palestine. A majority of seven recommended
also that Palestine be partitioned into two separate states,
one Arab, one Jewish, united economically. Three members—from India, Iran, and Yugoslavia—opposed partition and recommended Arab and Jewish provinces, under a Federal government which would control immigra-

tion and political policies. How they thought they could make that arrangement work was left unexplained.

The Assembly passed over to another committee (designated the Ad Hoc Committee) the task of determining how the majority recommendations could or should be carried into effect. Arthur Creech-Jones, Britain's Colonial Secretary, put the Committee on notice that the British Government, while accepting the majority report, would not use its troops to do so unless both Arabs and Jews agreed to the proposed solution.[6] The Russian and Polish members praised the majority report, favored permission for Jews to enter Palestine, and even deplored Arab threats. They were out to corner Britain—and by doing so made Bevin more frenetically anti-Communist.

The American Government hesitated. But the obstinacy of the Arab leaders, and their belligerence, incensed Truman. As instructed, Herschel Johnson, the Deputy American representative on the Ad Hoc Committee, announced on October 11 that the American Government would support the basic principles of the UNSCOP report and the majority recommendations in regard to partition and immigration. But, he added, it thought several territorial changes should be made in order to give effect more accurately to the principles on which the plan was based. Chief among these was that the Negev, the southern section of Palestine, then a wasteland, which UNSCOP had awarded to the Jewish state, be left in Arab hands, and the Jaffa and its environs, in which many thousands of Arabs lived, should also be excluded from the Jewish state. With reason the Jewish Agency inferred this American proposal was due to a wish to placate Britain, and influenced by the strategic importance of Negev.

Among the other members of the Ad Hoc Committee

who favored partition were Semyon Tsarapkin of Russia, Lester Pearson of Canada, Jorge Garcia-Granados of Guatemala, all mentally adroit, word-gifted men. But they differed about the time and way in which the UNSCOP program should be carried into effect. Johnson was still trying to enlist British cooperation in the effectuation of the partition plan. Tsarapkin was impatiently advocating that the Mandate be terminated at once; he visualized subsequent arrangements which would have accorded the Soviet Union an indefinitely prolonged chance to interfere in Palestine affairs—through either the Security Council or UN peace-keeping forces.

Wearily, in November, arguments drained but passions not spent, the Ad Hoc Committee considered a complicated compromise. This involved the withdrawal of British forces on May 1, 1948 and only two months of transition thereafter before the creation of two independent states. These steps, and the contemplated democratic elections for two constituent assemblies to form two provisional governments were to be supervised by a UN Commission.[7]

The British Government was by then eager to give up the Mandate. Various members of the British Cabinet were becoming tired of the burden and the anathema. Sir Stafford Cripps, who had succeeded Dalton as Chancellor of the Exchequer, thought the costs outweighed the benefits.[8] Then there was the example of India— where, it was thought, that following the enactment of the Independence Bill the previous July, two hostile communities—one Moslem, one Hindu—were managing to settle their affairs.

But the British Government would not assent to the proposed procedure and schedule for partitioning. On

November 13, Sir Alexander Cadogan, at a session of the Ad Hoc Committee convened at British request, declared flatly that the British Government would give up the Mandate on May 1 next, and evacuate its forces by August 1 next. But before then it would not permit interference and it would not cooperate in the effectuation of the partition plan. As long as British forces were in Palestine they would maintain law and order; they would not turn over any authority to the UN Commission until "the time came." The Zionists suspected that the British were going to manage the evacuation of military installations and vantage points in a manner that would enable the Arab forces to take them over. Their past experience caused them to anticipate the worst.

The British stance at this juncture could be construed as a challenge to the United States to take on the job of implementing the UNSCOP report alone or jointly, if it chose, with the Soviet Union.

The decisive climax was at hand. Would two-thirds of the members of the Assembly vote for acceptance of the partition plan—in the face of the combined opposition of the Arab (or would it be all Moslem countries?) and British (or would it be all the members of the British Commonwealth)?

Truman announced that the American Government would support the plan, and that meant many nations in the Assembly would follow the American lead. The Zionists took American support more or less for granted, and concentrated their fire instead on an amendment which the American representative in the Assembly advanced—presumably after clearance at the White House. It was that a large part of the Negev—its important south-

ern section—be taken out of the prospective Jewish state
and incorporated in the prospective Arab state. Agitated,
Weizmann asked Truman to see him. When he did on
November 19, the imaginative scientist conveyed to the
President his hopeful conception of what the Jews could
make of the Negev. If they brought water, explored its
minerals, located industries, why could not the whole
Palestinian region be made, by Jewish diligence and skill,
and Western technology, to bloom again; to be productive
enough to support many millions of people as it had, once
upon a time? The vision convinced or captured the President. He at once telephoned Johnson to forget the American amendment and support the inclusion of the Negev in
the Jewish state.

During the succeeding last days of discussion, after
the United States and the Soviet Union had reached a
compromise regarding the roles of the Assembly and the
Security Council in the implementation of the partition
plan, Johnson made a fervent plea, saying, "The governments who believe in partition think it is not perfect but
that it is humanly just and workable and if adopted will
make a genuine contribution to the solution of one of the
most thorny political problems of the world today . . ."

Early in the debate Secretary of State George C. Marshall, in his address to the Assembly, said that "great
weight" should be given to the recommendations of
UNSCOP. Truman, in his *Memoirs*, related that "Some
Zionist leaders were even suggesting that we pressure
sovereign nations into favorable votes in the General
Assembly." Instead of directly denying that the American
Government did so, he resorted to a generalization which
may or may not suit the case, "I have never approved of
the practice of the strong imposing their will on the weak,
whether among men or among nations." [9] Although the

President and Secretary Marshall did not exert themselves
personally in behalf of the partition plan, it was widely
believed—and with valid reason—at the time that his
subordinates in the White House and his political as-
sociates did; it has since become known that some of them
[10]

concurrently Arab leaders, especially Ibn Saud, re-
to Roosevelt's promise, were warning Truman
separate Jewish state were established, the Arabs
take to arms, and the war would be long and
, and in the end the Jewish state would be isolated
would perish.

At this juncture there were two conflicting sources of
authority, giving different instructions to the American
representative on UNSCOP and the Assembly. Secretary
Marshall had refused, as far as it was possible, to concern
himself with the Palestine problem. Its direction was en-
trusted to the Under-Secretary, Robert L. Lovett, who
trusted the usual operations to the Near East Division
under Loy Henderson. Henderson was a permanent and
veteran foreign service officer whose career, it was thought,
need not be blighted by blame for unpopular decisions.

During this wrought-up period, Henderson was told
by Lovett that he might—or should—inform the ambassadors of the Arab countries that the American Government was going to vote for the partition resolution but
would not bring pressure on other UN members to do so.
Henderson gave this assurance to the Arab representatives
in Washington and informed Johnson accordingly. But
even as he was doing so, David Niles, an administrative
assistant to the President, was, by telephone, instructing
Johnson to use any and all sorts of persuasion and in-
ducement to win votes for the Resolution, and directly

conveying the wish of the White House to those members of the Assembly who were susceptible. It is not surprising that Herschel Johnson was distraught.

Despite the endeavors of the White House, the number of members of the Assembly who were likely to oppose or abstain might be large enough to prevent the necessary two-thirds vote of approval. Under the circumstances, the votes of the Communist countries became crucial. The Soviet Government had postponed revelation of its decision. Hence the great, the joyous relief of the representatives of the Jewish Agency when, one evening, Ambassador Tsarapkin, after quizzing them in private conversation, said his Government would support the Zionist cause. This the Soviets did, unequivocally, to the delighted surprise of the Zionists.[11] "What's happened to us in connection with the Soviet Union is a real miracle," it seemed to Moshe Shertok, leader of the Jewish group.[12] Well it might have seemed. In not one other of the many current international disputes were the United States and the Soviet Union aligned on the same side.

As a result of discussion in the Assembly, certain details of the plan had been changed; the size of the proposed Jewish state was somewhat reduced, Jaffa was transferred to the Arab state as was also a sizable part of the Negev near the Mediterranean and Egyptian frontiers. These were to become the scene of action during the Suez campaign in 1956 and the Israeli-Arab war in 1967.

On the 29th of November, amid tense excitement, the vote was finally taken. Thirty-three members voted for the Resolution to partition, thirteen opposed it, ten members did not vote. The Zionist Jews in and out of Palestine rejoiced.[13] The Arab representatives announced that they would not abide by the Resolution.

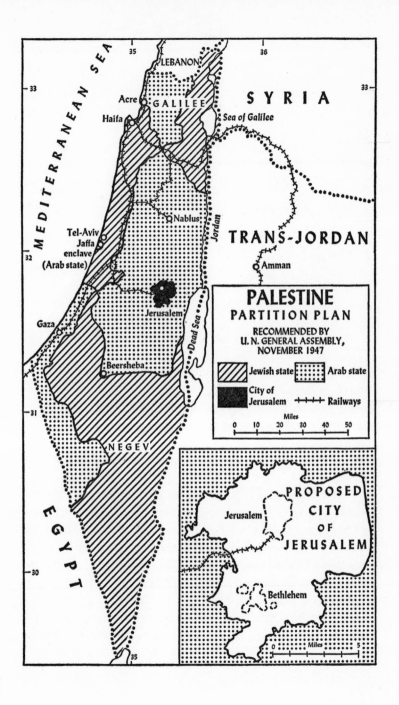

MEDITERRANEAN SEA

LEBANON

Acre
GALILEE
Haifa
Sea of Galilee

S Y R I A

Nablus

Jordan

TRANS-JORDAN

Tel-Aviv
Jaffa
enclave
(Arab state)

Amman

Gaza

Jerusalem

Dead Sea

Beersheba

N E G E V

E G Y P T

PALESTINE
PARTITION PLAN
RECOMMENDED BY
U. N. GENERAL ASSEMBLY,
NOVEMBER 1947

Jewish state · Arab state

City of
Jerusalem · Railways

Miles

0   10   20   30   40   50

PROPOSED
CITY
OF
JERUSALEM

Jerusalem

Bethlehem

0   Miles   5

4

❮❮❮-❮❮❮-❮❮❮-❮❮❮-❮❮❮-

But How Could Partition Be Effected?

How, THEN, was partition to be carried into effect? Those who had argued with both the Arabs and the Jews were dubious whether, even though both the United States and Russia had supported the partition plan, it could be carried out unless imposed by force. To the Security Council the resolution assigned the problem of devising the measures necessary to implement the plan by August 1, 1948, when British forces were to evacuate the country.

The British Government was not reconciled to the partition plan. In the course of a two-day debate in the House of Commons (on December 11 and 12), Bevin announced that "We have no intention of opposing that decision [for partition] but we cannot ourselves undertake, either individually or collectively in association with others, to impose the decision by force." This was correctly taken to mean that the British Government would not cooperate even in the creation of a United Nations police force in

Palestine. It wanted out, resentful of the way in which other Western countries, by refusing to open their gates widely to Jewish immigration, had concentrated the tide on Palestine and nurtured a situation which was causing it to quit the country. Ignoring British contentions that any new policy should be complemented by provisions for enforcement, they had gone ahead with the program for partition. Then let the sponsors find out a way of preventing civil war, and if they could not, let war come! Probably the thought of the aggrieved officials in the War Office, Foreign and Colonial Offices, went further. Some might have been confident, wishfully confident, despite expert judgment to the contrary, that the Arabs would be able to smash the Jewish community of Palestine.

During the months after the adoption of the UN resolution to partition Palestine, the British Government stumbled about, while adhering to its resolve to be clear of Palestine. At this time, it ought to be recalled, Britain, enabled by the Marshall Plan to recover from the awful winter of 1946–47, was facing the hardships of still another winter.

Elizabeth Monroe's interpretation of the reasons why British policy during this period—the winter of 1947–48—became so disjunctive is probably near the mark.

> . . . *Three . . . British departments were divesting themselves of responsibility on Palestine—the Colonial Office, the War Office, and the Foreign Office. The first wanted to salvage some of its handiwork from the wreckage; the second wanted to extricate its men and material intact; the third, to keep up the British position in the Western world.*[1]

The result was confusion, and loss of control and morale. Attlee was, to the end of his life, compelled to deny that the Government allowed organized chaos to come with the hopeful thought that the Arabs would prevail.

The American authorities became more uneasy over the way in which relations with Britain were being nicked by the sharp differences over Palestine, by mounting mistrust of the Soviet reasons for favoring partition, and by a flare-up of anxiety over the possible consequences of alienating the Moslem countries.

The sense that differences over Palestine should not be allowed to spoil the vital American association with Britain was deepened by the abrasive break with the Soviet Government over Germany which occurred at the meeting of the Council of Foreign Ministers in London in December 1947. From then on, no matter how vehement the Russian protests, the three Western occupying powers were determined to proceed to establish an independent democratic West German state allied with them.

Continued experience was nurturing suspicions that the Russians' purposes for favoring partition of Palestine were malevolent. Did not—the query hung in the air like a red lantern—the Soviet officials think thereby to gain entry into the Middle East, perhaps by participation in a UN force, and by taking advantage of the chaos and conflict that might result in the Middle East? It is possible also that the pro-Zionist position that the Russians had adopted suddenly gave more credence, though no more authenticity, to the prediction that a Jewish state would be Communistically inclined. This opinion, sedulously spread by the opponents of Zionism, Weizmann deemed so harmful to the Zionist cause that he wrote a letter to Truman just to deny the allegation.

In the face of these suspicions, the military strategists, led by Defense Secretary James Forrestal and the President's representative on the Chiefs of Staff, Admiral William Leahy, began to get a better hearing for their emphasis on the strategic importance of the oil of the Middle East and of air bases in Palestine.[2]

Henderson and his colleagues in the State Department and American ambassadors in the Arab countries were dismayed at the possibility that, in order to prevent the extinction of Israel, the United States might become engaged in a war against the Arabs—against the Arab contingents trained and equipped by the British—while the Communists waited for their chance to benefit.

While these several gusts of anxiety were circulating around the White House, it was becoming more evident that the partition plan could not be carried out unless some stronger military forces, either national or international, took command in Palestine. Truman and his advisers, both civilian and military, decisively dismissed the idea that the United States would provide the necessary forces alone; and they were hesitant, at this time, even about providing a contingent for an international force because the Russians would provide a similar one. Within the Assembly the idea was advanced of a UN force composed exclusively of contingents from the middle and smaller powers. But this project became lost in the tangled brushwood of controversy in the Assembly.

Faced with this impasse, the UN Committee which had been trying to find the modes for carrying out the resolution for partition reported to the Security Council that it would not be able to discharge its responsibilities when the Mandate ended, without armed assistance.

The President was as stumped as the Committee. He

did not want to obligate the American Government to the use of force in order to carry out the program. This was indicated by the statement which Warren Austin made on February 24 in the Security Council. He made a distinction between a "UN recommendation" and a "UN decision." The partition resolution was, in the American view, a recommendation, and this meant that there was no obligation to use force to carry it out. "The Council's action," Austin said, "in other words, is directed to keeping the peace, not enforcing partition."

Truman, at this juncture, felt that he was being unfairly and excessively pushed and prodded by the Zionist Jews to act in their behalf. His temper is suggested by a passage in his *Memoirs,* in which he recalls that "Individuals and groups asked me usually in rather quarrelsome and emotional ways to stop the Arabs, to keep the British from supporting the Arabs, to furnish American soldiers, to do this, that the other." [3] So keen was his resentment that he resolved that he would not talk again with any spokesman for the Zionist cause.

The President's annoyance and worry at the way in which the Palestine situation was being forced upon his attention was accentuated in that crucial month of March 1948. General Lucius Clay, Commander of the American occupation forces in Germany, sensing that some new Soviet initiative was about to be taken, sent a telegram that set off alarm bells in Washington.

In these circumstances the American Government maintained an arms embargo for the Middle East even though it knew that the Arab states were providing arms for the complotters in Palestine.

At this juncture there occurred one of those crinkles in Truman's course, the timing of which is hard to explain, and the intent of which is smudged by fading and contradictory memories.

Some days or weeks previously, there had been composed in the State Department an announcement to be made in the Security Council that the American Government thought that the effort to go forward with the plan of partition should be suspended and a temporary Trusteeship created. Lovett had approved it. Henderson understood—presumably from what Lovett said—that the President also had. Whether the President actually read all or part of it is not known. But the word passed down was that the State Department should choose the time when the Ambassador to the UN was to inform the Security Council of our recoil. Austin had been advised by the State Department—by whom is not of record, but instructions to Austin were usually telephoned via Lovett's office, via Assistant Secretary of State for International Organization Affairs, Dean Rusk—to present it on or about March 18.

Presumably, the President, in this interval, had either forgotten that he had approved the statement, or failed to foresee how it would be construed and what a stir it would cause.[4]

Weizmann had some days before sought another chance to talk with the President. He had been told that for the time being neither he nor any other Zionist spokesman would be heard. But on March 13, Eddie Jacobson, Truman's pal in the First World War and his former partner in the haberdashery business, interceded. Truman, by his own account, said at first he wouldn't discuss Palestine even with Weizmann, since it would cause more "wrong interpretations." According to Jacobson's reminiscent account, as soon as he brought up the subject of Palestine, the President had become tense in appearance and abrupt and bitter in speech; and he made it almost impossible for Jacobson to continue, when he said sharply ". . . that he didn't want to discuss Palestine or the Jews or the Arabs or the British; that he was satisfied to let these subjects take their course through the United Nations." [5] But Jacobson had continued to plead with him to down his resentment at the mean and disrespectful accusations of some of the Zionist leaders and to see Weizmann, the wisest and most moderate of them—who, an old man and a very sick one, had made the long journey to the United States in the hope of being able to get American support at this crucial juncture. Again, according to Jacobson, after all arguments had failed, he appealed to Truman to live up to his own idol, Andrew Jackson. And the President, after a long pause, had swung around and said, "You win, you bald-headed. . . . I will see him. Tell Matt [Matt Connelly, his Appointment Secretary] to arrange a meeting as soon as possible after I return from New York on March 17."

The general outlook in the President's mind is shown in the message which he sent to Congress on that day, March 17, urging it to pass pending legislation for the fulfillment of the Marshall program and the enactment of universal military training and the restoration of a Selective Service Act. His condemnation of Communism was made even more explicit in an address that he gave in New York that night.

On that same day, the five Foreign Ministers of Western European democracies had signed the treaty of Brussels, and the President had said in his speech, "I am sure that the determination of the free countries of Europe to protect themselves will be matched by an equal determination on our part to help them protect themselves." The Communist coup in Czechoslovakia—in late February—was ringing in his thoughts.

But although the Palestine question seemed to him at this time of only secondary importance and a nagging irritant, he kept his word and received Weizmann, as arranged, on March 18th.

With echoes of Truman's speech of the night before still resounding, the two men talked for almost three-quarters of an hour. The visitor from Palestine, doing most of the talking, stressed again the importance of the Negev area in the south to any Jewish state. In his *Memoirs* the President does not tell what was said and promised. Rather laconically he records merely that he explained the basis of his interest in the Jewish problem, that his primary concern was to see justice done, and that "I felt that he [Weizmann] had reached a full understanding of my policy and that I knew what it was that he wanted." [6] Jacobson recounts that one of the Zionist representatives who had accompanied Weizmann to Washington telephoned to let him know that Weizmann was "happy and gratified," and that in practically no time he (Jacobson) found out that Truman had pledged his word that the Negev would be and remain part of the Jewish state. [7]

Both accounts, and Weizmann's brief reference to the meeting in his *Memoirs,* leave us still to wonder whether the President was definite in any other respect. All signs indicate that he did not spoil Weizmann's pleasure in his expression of sympathetic support by telling him of the astounding change in tactics—or policy—which Austin was to announce in the Security Council the very next day—the 19th.

Austin proposed that since no way had yet been found to carry out the partition resolution peacefully, the attempt should be suspended. In order to maintain the peace and afford further opportunity to seek agreement, he suggested that a special session of the Assembly be called to establish a temporary trusteeship under the Trusteeship Council, when on May 15 the Mandate was to end.

Truman then and subsequently denied that this was a shift in American policy—or even a marked swerve. In his *Memoirs* he holds that, "This was not a rejection of partition but rather an effort to postpone its effective date until proper conditions for the establishment of self-government in the two parts might be established." [8]

Shift or makeshift—swerve or turn—Secretary Marshall took responsibility for the change in American policy. He said in a public statement on March 20, "I recommended it to the President and he approved my recommendation. The primary and overriding consideration . . . is the need to maintain the peace." Similarly, at Hearings of the Armed Service Committee of the Senate, taking heed of the quick surge of criticism of Austin's declaration, he explained that the grave current international crisis made it most important to prevent open war in Palestine, but that unless some emergency action was taken there would be widespread fighting in the Holy Land. Therefore, some measure which would create in Palestine a public authority capable of preventing war was essential; the Trusteeship proposed, he said, was advanced to deal with this necessity.

On the same day, March 20—it was no chance coincidence—after stormy argument when Western members of the Control Council for Germany refused to discuss their plans for Germany, the Soviet member, Marshal Vassily Sokolovsky, stalked out of the meeting. Marshall and other military advisers, it should be added, had told the President that in the event of trouble in Palestine, the United States could send only token forces there. They also were disturbed because if there was war in Palestine, the flow of Middle Eastern oil to Europe, needed to go forward with the Marshall Plan program, might be disrupted.

The Russian representative on the Security Council had charged at once that the United States was willing to jettison the partition plan because of the interest in Middle Eastern oil and strategic calculations. And Bevin said in the House of Commons on March 23, "I do want to emphasize that we have to get into a position to enable us to be out of Palestine. That is the fundamental point of British policy."

Harassed by the pro-Zionists and called traitor and hypocrite by the most hot-headed among them, the President on March 25 flatly averred that unfortunately, it had become clear that the partition plan could not be carried out by peaceful means. He said the U.S. could not undertake to impose this solution upon the people of Palestine by use of American troops both on [UN] Charter grounds and as a matter of national policy. Trusteeship was not proposed as a substitute for the partition plan but as an effort to fill the vacuum created by the termination of the Mandate on May 15. The President added, "In order to avert tragedy in Palestine an immediate truce must be reached between the Arabs and Jews of that country." How often has this exhortation been heard in subsequent times?

However, the President in this interim was bothered

by the thought that Weizmann might believe he had been deceived and that he (the President) had broken his word. Therefore, he had asked his general counsel, Samuel Rosenman, on March 20, to assure Weizmann ". . . that there was not and would not be any change in the long [sic] policy he and I had talked about." [9] Rosenman did so. And on the 23rd Weizmann undertook to comfort Jacobson by telephone, telling him, in what Jacobson avers in his memo was word for word,

> *Don't be disappointed and do not feel badly. I do not believe that President Truman knew what was going to happen in the United Nations on Friday [the 19th] when he talked to me the day before. . . . Don't forget for a single moment that Harry S. Truman is the most powerful single man in the world. You have a job to do: so keep the White House doors open.*[10]

Truman has recalled with appreciation that Weizmann was one of the few prominent Zionists who did not castigate him. "He knew, I am sure," the President later commented, "what the direction of American policy really was." [11] What it turned out to be after the alarms of March ebbed!

However, in that immediate present, the American representatives sedulously sought support of other members of the Assembly for the Trusteeship proposal. At a special session of the Assembly, convened on April 16, the American delegation again appealed for a temporary Trusteeship. But to no avail. The Soviet representative still supported the partition plan; the British representative, Creech-Jones, argued that there was not enough time left to establish a UN Trusteeship. No agreement had been reached on the main issues that would have faced the Trusteeship at once—what should be done about immigration, land settlement, and the importation of arms. He suggested instead that some "neutral authority" be set up to seek a settlement by mediation. Austin called on Weizmann in an effort to impress him with the danger the Palestine Jews would be in unless protected by a Trusteeship. But Weizmann thought they could cope with the Arab armies.

These efforts having come to naught, Truman thereafter let events take their course. But he had apparently by then made up his mind, secretly and stubbornly, that if no interim arrangement for the government of Palestine was established when on May 15 (May 14, Washington time) the British forces left Palestine, and the Jews proclaimed a National State, the American Government would recognize it. For, on April 12, when Jacobson, having just talked with Weizmann, called on the President again, Truman authorized him to tell Weizmann that he stood by the promise he had made; and he agreed with Jacobson that the American Government should recognize the new Jewish state if and when it came into existence. Whether this affirmation was relayed to Weizmann, and by him relayed to Palestine, and whether it may have influenced the course of the Palestinian Zionists before and during the mid-May climax, is still not known.

5

𝕶𝕶𝕶-𝕶𝕶𝕶-𝕶𝕶𝕶-𝕶𝕶𝕶-𝕶𝕶𝕶-

War and Birth

As THE DAY of departure of the British forces neared, none could doubt that there would be a war between the Jews and the Arabs. Zionist terrorism had been spreading and becoming more unsparing of both British and Arabs. Other Arab countries threatened to invade Palestine when the time came. In many towns and villages fighting had already begun. Its issue was uncertain.

The Zionist leaders felt that the time had arrived to take the risk and face the danger and disregard all warnings against precipitate action. David Ben Gurion, Chairman of the Executive Group of the Zionist Organization, turned for last-minute advice to Weizmann, who was at Nice, and the message returned was "Proclaim the State no matter what ensues."

On the 13th Weizmann notified the President that the Jews of Palestine were determined to proclaim their state at midnight on the 14th. Truman called into consultation Secretary of State Marshall, Under-Secretary Lovett, Clark Clifford, his legal counsel, David Niles, his administrative assistant, and several others. Marshall thought the American Government, before deciding how to act, should con-

fer with the British and French Governments. But Truman
did not wish to procrastinate. He instructed Clifford to
get in touch with Eliahu Epstein, the representative of
the Jewish Agency in Washington, so they might co-
ordinate the action in mind.

Epstein at once submitted a formal request for recognition *within the boundaries* of the UN resolution of November 29, 1947. The name *Israel* was a last-minute selection
of the Jewish Agency; until then the favored designation
had been "State of the Jews" after Theodore Herzl's book.
The President instructed his Press Secretary at once to
announce that the American Government would give de
facto recognition of the new Jewish state; and the announcement was on the air only eleven minutes after that
state had declared its independence in Tel-Aviv.[1]

It may be surmised that the two main reasons for this
haste was the wish to assure the enthusiastic favor of
American Jews and the wish to be first to grant recognition, especially to be ahead of the Soviet Union. But a
reading of the President's *Memoirs* suggests that he felt
the more satisfaction in his action because finally he was
besting those officials of the State Department and the
Foreign Office who had tried so hard to circumvent him.
They were upset by his swift action, but whether they
were informed in advance is disputed.

In his *Memoirs* the President wrote, "I was told that to
some of the career men in the State Department this announcement came as a surprise." [2] Loy Henderson, in discussing the event, has said that actually he and members
of his division had composed the letter of recognition.[3]
The American representatives in the UN seem, however,
to have been taken aback.

Ambassador Gromyko indicated that Russia planned to

recognize the Jewish state but he accused the American Government of plunging the UN into a "ludicrous situation" by its sudden act. The Soviet Government granted formal recognition of the new state a few days later.

At once the President had to face a barrage of alarming comments from American ambassadors in the Arab countries of the Middle East. Typical was the warning sent by Pinckney Tuck, the Ambassador in Egypt, that this action would prolong conflict in Palestine and jeopardize national security. Their main fear was the same as that of their colleagues in the State Department, that the war in Palestine would give the Soviet Union a good chance to intervene; possibly to send troops into the Middle East, certainly to make friends with the Arabs and persuade them to eject American oil interests. Most American diplomats advised against lifting the embargo on the shipment of arms to Israel.

For the time being this became a crucial issue. The Arabs of Palestine and the invading Arabs were deemed to be well equipped with British arms, while the arsenal of the Jews was small. However, near the day of partition they received shipments of arms, not from the United States but from Czechoslovakia. Their purchase had been arranged by representatives of the Haganah, and the bargain had been completed after the Czechs were assured that the Soviet Government had no objection. Once again Jacobson was asked by the ailing Weizmann to try to see the President again and discuss with him the arms embargo. When he did so on May 15, he gave the President details about how the Arabs were being armed by the British, and expressed the opinion that the British seemed to wish to see the new state of Israel destroyed. The President listened carefully but gave no definite promise.

Similarly he refrained from making any definite response to another request which Jacobson, at Weizmann's request, put before him—the possibility of granting Israel a loan of $100,000,000. Shortly afterwards Truman made manifest his sympathetic support of the new state by inviting Weizmann, who had been named the first President of Israel, to come and see him before he left for home. Weizmann went to Washington and stayed at Blair House as the guest of the President. He reported to an intermediary that he was "sailing with a light heart and was a very happy man."

The act of recognition sustained the morale of the new state. But, of course, it did not determine whether it could survive.

The Jews in Israel had been fighting not only Palestinian Arabs but contingents of Arab volunteers from Syria, Iraq and Trans-Jordan who had begun to infiltrate soon after the Assembly Resolution for partition. Under the command of Fawzi Kaukyi, a Syrian, they formed the Palestine Liberation Army. The British authorities had not prevented or interfered with this Arab incursion. The arsenal of the Jews was small, even after it received the first shipment of arms from Czechoslovakia in May 1948; they had no heavy artillery, armored cars, tanks, or planes. But still they beat off Arab attacks on the Jewish settlements, and late in April trounced Arab forces in the important city of Haifa—after which the 65,000 Arabs fled, leaving the city to its 80,000 Jews. During May the Arab exodus was widespread, stimulated by fears of Jewish reprisals and stories of Jewish brutality. The Arab armies, then including 12,000 Egyptian troops, marched toward Haifa and Tel-Aviv and Jerusalem. Their leaders sped them along by predictions that the war over Palestine would be ended in ten days. But it was not.

A committee of the UN Assembly appointed the Swedish Count Folke Bernadotte as its mediator to go to Palestine and seek to bring about an immediate truce and then a peaceful settlement. The American Government had advocated this measure. In doing so it was aligned with the Soviet authorities against sullen British and Arab objections. These attempts went on most earnestly through the summer of 1948, as Berlin was being enclosed in a Communist grip. Informed observers, in the know, believe that in this period the managers of Britain's partisan Palestine policy may have shared the confidence of the Arabs that they would win and crush the new state of Israel. True, the General Officer commanding the British forces in Palestine had testified before a plenary meeting of the Anglo-American Commission a year before that he thought the Haganah would be able without difficulty to hold any area allocated to the Jews under partition, whereas large British contingents would be required to police any solution which involved the suppression of the Haganah. But the member of the Commission who disclosed this fact, Richard Crossman, has averred that, "This was the only evidence proffered to us which was struck from the record as too secret to be recorded. Hence I was never able to present it to Mr. Attlee or Mr. Bevin." [4] Bevin resolutely rejected suggestions that Britain should recognize the state of Israel even though the UN mediator was negotiating with its leaders.

The eventual settlement was determined by military success and failure rather than by diplomatic activity; the prolonged, stale, and tired last exertions of the diplomats proved of no further consequence.

But we ought to emboss in the record a summary nota-
tion on the nobly-purposed but poorly-gauged proposals
of Bernadotte, and his tragic death. Bernadotte's formula
envisaged changes in the partition plan to the disadvan-
tage of Israel, and a territorial division less favorable than
that achieved by the Zionist forces by the middle of
summer. Still, when the United Nations met in Paris in
September, Marshall, at this time vitally linked with Bevin
in resistance to the blockade of Berlin, joined in endorsing
Bernadotte's latest proposals (in his report presented post-
humously to the UN General Assembly in Paris on September 20), as "fair and sound." It was made known that
the State Department thought well of the plan.[5]

The Russian propagandists turned their guns on the
United States—alleging that it was conniving in Bernadotte's tactics, which were designed to favor Trans-Jordan
as a British puppet and hub of British plans to build a
great Arab combination.[6] What would have happened,
had not Jewish terrorists assassinated Bernadotte (in
Jerusalem on September 17), cannot be known.[7] But
probably this proposal like its predecessors would have
withered in the heat of war.

Despite their opinion that Bernadotte was against them,
virtually all members of the Jewish community in Israel
heard the news of his assassination with horror. In the
words of a contemporary observer, "everyone [in Israel]
seemed to feel that the bullet that riddled the mediator's
body had torn into the state's own precarious texture." [8]
Expressions of shock and sorrow poured in from everywhere. Arab regret was perhaps palliated by the sense
that the event would hurt the Israeli cause; while the
Zionists were anxious to dispel suspicion of moral—if not
physical—complicity in the assassination. The perpetrators

of the crime, despite a widespread search by the Government of Israel, were never caught, but were generally known to be members of a splinter group of underground extremists.[9]

Truman, by then launched on his stalwart campaign for re-election, was mindful that the platform of the Democratic Party expressed approval of the original UN partition resolution and contained a promise to oppose any territorial changes to which Israel would not agree. He had the impulse to make a public statement reaffirming his resolve to be faithful to this profession of policy. After talking with Marshall, he decided, however, not to crowd Britain and the Arabs harder at this time.

But Truman's hand was forced by the Republican rival for the Presidency, Thomas E. Dewey, who had no recalcitrant State Department or Joint Chiefs of Staff to consider. The former Governor of New York accused Truman of defaulting on Democratic Party promises to Israel. With election day less than two weeks away the President, on October 24, issued a statement saying that the Bernadotte plan was merely "a basis for" new negotiations; and Acting Secretary of State Lovett let the press know that the President had not told Marshall in advance of the statement. Then in the course of a combative speech at Madison Square Garden in New York City on October 28, he came out openly for Israel and against the Bernadotte proposals which still had many sponsors in the UN. "Israel," he said, "must be large enough and strong enough to make its people self-supporting and secure." [10]

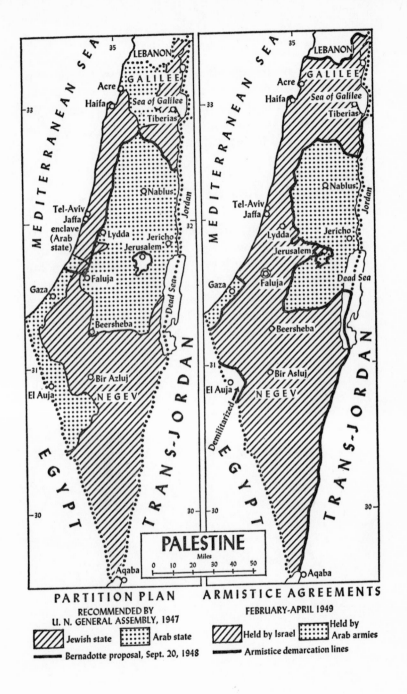

PALESTINE

Miles
0   10   20   30   40   50

PARTITION PLAN
RECOMMENDED BY
U. N. GENERAL ASSEMBLY, 1947

//// Jewish state   :::: Arab state

■■■ Bernadotte proposal, Sept. 20, 1948

ARMISTICE AGREEMENTS
FEBRUARY-APRIL 1949

//// Held by Israel   :::: Held by Arab armies

■■■ Armistice demarcation lines

Truman won the election. The American Government supported the application of the new state of Israel for admission into the UN, as did the Soviet Government. But so many of the members abstained from taking sides that this decision had to be postponed.[10]

By the end of 1948 the Government of the state of Israel was operating well. The territory controlled by its armies was somewhat larger than what had been accorded in the original partition plan. No independent Arab state in Palestine was coming into existence because so many Arabs had fled, mostly to the adjoining Arab state of Trans-Jordan, which incorporated into its territory the central area of Palestine that had been designated as the main realm of a Palestinian Arab state.

The Still-Clouded Future

THE DIPLOMATS of the United States and the Soviet Union were the first to arrive in Israel early in August 1948. Both lived in the same hotel in Tel-Aviv. Thus, for a short time, the Stars and Stripes and the Hammer and Sickle were flown side by side in an Israeli city. But this was a singular conjunction of quite different purposes, not a symbol of association. The two countries opposed each other everywhere else. The birth of Israel occurred outside of the main arenas of struggle. It was one of those episodes illustrative of Sir Edward Grey's aphorism—that diplomacy did not make events; rather events made diplomacy.

Britain's prestige in the Middle East was greatly impaired. She had striven hard to appease her Arab friends and affiliates, but they had performed poorly in the test of battle. Russian diplomacy could consider itself successful, but the Zionists felt the victory was theirs, not Stalin's. Neither the Jews of Palestine nor the Arab countries really trusted Soviet purposes. The American Government could rightly take pride in having been at critical times a protector of Zionist ambitions, without spoiling the American relationship with Britain on any other vital matters, or losing American ownership of the vast oil fields of the Middle East.

The birth of Israel was in a tousled bed, circled by enemies who wished it to die. Time has proven how hardy it is. But alas, the hate of the Arab neighbors has lasted. A craving for reparations and vengeance still governs their spirits, incited by prophecies that Israel will yet be destroyed. American diplomacy in the Middle East cannot be deployed on the comfortable thought that the future of Israel is assured.

A President of the United States someday may confront a situation in the Middle East as tense and twisted as that which tried Truman and the American people in 1947–1948. For the present only force and fear keep the peace there. But the intrusion of atomic weapons makes the oil and bases of the Middle East less dependable factors in the economy or strategy of any of the great powers. And technology enlarges the potential benefits to both Jews and Arabs of a true and firm peace. These evolving facts may ease the task of diplomacy—smooth out the tousled bed. If only out of some burning bush (or White House or Whitehall) there could come a decalogue by which both Jews and Arabs would abide.

Notes

I "A National Home for the Jewish People"

1) See the account written by Balfour's niece, Blanche E. C. Dugdale, *Arthur James Balfour*, New York, G. P. Putnam's Sons, 1937, Vol. II, p. 155. Other Cabinet members sympathetic to Zionism were the Prime Minister Lloyd George, General Smuts and Lord Milner. The permanent officials in the Foreign Office and War Office were at this time much in favor of the Declaration to enlist Jewish, particularly Zionist, help in the war effort, to thwart German bids for support of the Zionists, and in the hope of inducing Russian Jews to stop the drift to the left and keep Russia in the war. See Leonard J. Stein, *The Balfour Declaration*, New York, Simon & Schuster, 1961.

2) Josephus Daniels in his introduction to Paul L. Hanna, *British Policy in Palestine*, Washington, D.C., American Council on Public Affairs, 1942.

3) Colonel Richard Meinertzhagen, *Middle East Diary, 1917–1956*, London, Cresset Press, 1959, pp. 8–9. Somewhat later in September 1918, Balfour used almost the same words in a letter he sent to Alfred Zimmern who was then working in the Political Section of the Foreign Office. But he explained that he thought it risky to discuss the subject at that time. The letter is reproduced and commented on by Carroll Quigley in "Lord Balfour's Personal Position in the Balfour Declaration," *Middle East Journal*, Summer 1968.

When, in June 1921, there was much discussion about partition and how to carry out the Declaration, which had been written into the Mandate for Palestine given by the League of Nations to Britain, Weizmann discussed its meaning with important members of the British Cabinet. Winston Churchill, then Secretary for the Colonies, strongly protested against Weizmann's views that the Declaration contemplated an ultimate Jewish majority in Palestine. But Lloyd George and Balfour agreed that the Declaration was intended to accord the Jews an opportunity to become a majority in an eventual Jewish state. See Meinertzhagen, *Middle East Diary,* p. 104.

Article 2 of the League of Nations Mandate instrument for Palestine made the Mandatory responsible for placing the country under such "political, administrative and economic conditions as will secure the establishment of the Jewish National Home . . . and the development of self-governing institutions."

4) *Statistical Abstract of Palestine, 1929,* Jerusalem, Karen Hayesod, 1930, p. 34.

5) General Marshall testified to the same effect. This meeting of the Committee on Foreign Relations was closed and the records have been kept closed.

6) Both the Republican and Democratic platforms contained planks to that effect. The pertinent paragraph in the Republican platform read, "In order to give refuge to millions of distressed Jewish men, women, and children driven from their homes by tyranny, we call for the opening of Palestine to their unrestricted immigration and land ownership, so that in accordance with the full intent and purpose of the Balfour Declaration of 1917 and a resolution of a Republican Congress in 1922, Palestine may be constituted as a free and democratic commonwealth. . . ."

The pertinent paragraph of the Democratic platform read, "We favor the opening of Palestine to unrestricted Jewish immigration and colonization, and such a policy is to result in the establishment there of a free and democratic Jewish commonwealth."

7) *The New York Times,* October 12, 1944.

8) *Ibid.* October 16, 1944.

II The British-American Effort

1) The deplorable history of the barriers maintained against these refugees from Hitler's terrorism and the sweep of war is told with thoroughness, fairness, and detachment in David S. Wyman's scholarly study, *Paper Walls*, Amherst, University of Massachusetts Press, 1968.

2) The Palestine Jewish Agency, which had been recognized under the terms of the Mandate as a public body to advise and cooperate with the Administration of Palestine, not only organized and coordinated the efforts of the Jews in Palestine, but served as the diplomatic agents of the yet unborn state. The Chairman of the Executive group of the Zionist Organization was also Chairman of the Executive body of the Jewish Agency. The lobbying, publicity, and fund-raising in the United States were conducted by the Zionist Organization of America and its subordinate American Zionist Emergency Council of which at this time Stephen Wise and Abba Hillel Silver were co-Chairmen.

3) The question of whether immigration was illegal, or whether the British Paper was illegal—as a violation of the Mandate—was vigorously argued, before and during the Hearings of the United Nations Special Commission on Palestine (UNSCOP). See also Norman Bentwich, *Israel*, New York, McGraw Hill, 1952.

4) Report to the Zionist Congress 1947–1948. The full story is told in Bracha Habas, *The Gate Breakers*, London, Herzl Press; New York, Thomas Yoseloff, 1963.

5) The latest edition of the Encyclopedia Britannica (Entry, *Palestine History*) gives the numbers as 678,000 Jews and 1,269,000 Arabs.

6) Quoted by Chaim Weizmann in his *Trial and Error*, New York, Harper, 1949, p. 549.

7) Bartley C. Crum, *Behind the Silken Curtain: A Personal Account of Anglo-American Diplomacy in Palestine and the Middle East*, New York, Simon and Schuster, 1947.

8) The British members of the Anglo-American Committee of Inquiry were:

1) Sir John Singleton (British Chairman), Judge of the High Court

2) Lord Robert Morrison, a Labour member of the House of Lords, former trade union leader and member of the House of Commons.

3) Richard Crossman, a young Labour member of the House of Commons who, during the Second World War, worked in the Foreign Office.

4) Major Reginald Manningham-Buller, a Conservative Member of Parliament.

5) Wilfred Crick, an economic adviser to the Bank of England.

6) Sir Frederick Liggett, an arbitrator in Labour management, former Deputy Secretary of the Ministry of Labour and National Services.

The American members were:

1) Judge Joseph C. Hutcheson (American Chairman), Judge of the Fifth Circuit Federal Court at Houston, a Texas Democrat.

2) James G. MacDonald, Former League of Nations High Commissioner for German refugees.

3) Frank W. Buxton, veteran editor of the *Boston Herald*.

4) Dr. Frank Aydelotte, Director of the Institute for Advanced Study at Princeton, and American Secretary of the Rhodes Trust.

5) William Phillips, Senior Foreign Service officer, a former Under-Secretary of State.

6) Bartley C. Crum, a San Francisco lawyer, a Willkie Republican who later supported Roosevelt.

My impression is that the American members were selected primarily because their experience, in common, might enable them to formulate a workable solution. But the composition of the English group was affected by a sense of the advisability or necessity of balancing off men from within Conservative political circles and men from within Labour political circles. The affiliations of the individual members did not significantly affect their activities or conclusions. The Labour Government was aggrieved later because the British members were deemed to have been too compliant to the judgment of the Americans.

9) Richard Crossman, *Palestine Mission,* New York, Harper, 1947, p. 77.

10) On May 7, 1946, the British Government offered to withdraw its forces from Egypt, subject to an alliance that would have made possible joint military arrangements. But the Egyptians were not satisfied.

For a brief account of British policy and problems in each country in this region, read Elizabeth Monroe's article, "Mr. Bevin's 'Arab Policy' " in *St. Anthony's Papers,* No. 11, 1961.

11) The history of illegal armed and terrorist organizations and activities in Palestine is one of many elements and variations, as were also their relations with the Zionist Agency and the British authorities in Palestine. It is impossible, without a long diversion from the main story of the course of diplomacy that led to the creation of Israel, to tell adequately and accurately of these illegal and violent activities, and of the British attempt to retaliate and repress them. Two good studies are Samuel Katz, *Days of Fire,* New York, Doubleday, 1968, and Menachem Begin, *The Revolt, Story of the Irgun,* Tel-Aviv, Hadar Publishing Company, 1964. London, Allen, 1951.

12) The same thought probably provided the witticism with which Bevin, when attending a reception at City Hall in New York City, replied to a young lady who accosted him and asked, "Why do you put them [the Jews] in Cyprus, why not the Waldorf Astoria Hotel?" (where Bevin and the British staff attending a meeting of the Council of Foreign Ministers were staying). Bevin answered, "Because there is no room, my dear." As noted in an entry in the Diary of Pierson Dixon, Bevin's secretary, November 7, 1946, contained in the book. *Double Diploma: The Life of Sir Pierson Dixon, Don and Diplomat,* by Pierson Dixon, London, Hutchinson, 1968.

13) Jon and David Kimche, *The Secret Roads: the Illegal Migration of a People, 1938–1948,* New York, Farrar, Straus, and Cudahy, 1955.

14) Giora Kulka, an Israeli graduate student in history at Harvard,

has written a note which recalls the daring character of the migration.

Britain had originally launched her anti-immigration campaign because she wished to prevent the Palestine Jewish community from growing to maturity and independence. From Britain's and the Arabs' point of view successful illegal immigration was dangerous. In the period between the end of the war and the creation of Israel sixty-five illegal immigrant ships arrived at the shores of Palestine. Compared with the thirteen ships which had made the run during the war, it was a veritable flood. The whole enterprise was now larger in scope, more skillfully organized, and filled with the suspense and danger of a cloak-and-dagger story. The highlight of this struggle became highly publicized in the world press and did much to win sympathy and diplomatic support for the Jews.

With every ship that the Mossad organizers rigged for the Palestine run, they acquired new experience in civil disobedience.

The first ship to make the headlines in the postwar period was the *Fede* which was being rigged for sailing in the small Italian port of La Spezia. In April 1946 some 1,000 refugees came on board, having been transported there in trucks "borrowed" from British Army Jewish units stationed in the area as part of the occupation forces. Soon, however, the British Army put the port area under siege, and the refugees on board the *Fede* responded by declaring a hunger strike. The Italian and world press was by now very much on the scene, and the populace of La Spezia, exhorted daily by the Mossad representative, made no secret of their hatred of the British, staging mass demonstrations and smashing windows in the Army offices in town.

The British were completely baffled by the weapon of desperation directed against them, and finally, after more than a month of siege, they gave in, permitting the *Fede* to leave for Palestine with all its passengers. Other ships were not so lucky. They were shadowed by British warships all the way from Europe and then, in Palestine territorial waters, rammed, boarded and seized. The scenes of hand-to-hand fighting, pelting British boarding parties with improvised hand-missiles of all sorts, gas bombing and the like repeated themselves with sickening regularity off the coast of the Holy Land. A few ships made it, their passengers being helped to shore at night by volunteers from nearby settlements; but many more were captured, and their human cargo transferred—amidst fierce scuffle—to prison ships and deported to Cyprus.

III   The United Nations Resolves on Partition

1) In fact Bevin's talks with the Jews were in a very preliminary stage. The Zionist Congress on December 9 repudiated the proposal and took such a rigid position that Weizmann resigned. See Harry Sacher, *The Establishment of a State*, London, G. Weidenfeld and Nicolson, 1952. New York, British Book Centre, 1952. The Arabs were just as dissatisfied.

2) Perhaps Secretary of State James Byrnes, during the meeting of the Council of Foreign Ministers in New York in November–December 1946, being in need of Bevin's support in his efforts to get Molotov to agree to some disputed provisions in the draft peace treaties with Italy and the German satellites, had told Bevin that the American Government was not going to press its demand for the admission of 100,000 Jews into Palestine. That is the implication of an entry which Sir Pierson Dixon, Bevin's private secretary, made in his Diary on December 15, 1946. Printed in *Double Diploma: The Life of Sir Pierson Dixon*, by Pierson Dixon.

3) Because of the unexpected and important influence Señor Jorge Garcia-Granados exercised in and on UNSCOP, I think it of enough historical interest to print in full a memorandum on the subject which Mr. Giora Kulka has written. While his information is derived mainly from Garcia-Granados's book, *The Birth of Israel*, New York, A. A. Knopf, 1948, he checked his statements with information in the records of the UNSCOP proceedings and records of the General Assembly for May 14, 1948 and *The New York Times*.

Jorge García-Granados was Guatemala's Ambassador to the United States and representative to the UN when he became a member of UNSCOP. From the very beginning he tended to regard the majority of his fellow-members as being tools in the "imperialistic" hands of the Anglo-American alliance. He persisted untiringly in his anti-British attitude, and he was generally supported by Enrique Rodríguez Fabregat of Uruguay, and more often than not by Jose Brilej of Yugoslavia. During UNSCOP's stay in Palestine he was involved in many battles over procedural points with the intention of making it clear that the UN authority was supreme over the British administration as far as the inquiry was concerned. He thought he was, however, consistently foiled by the majority of the members who regarded his activity as an unduly aggressive attempt to humiliate Great Britain.

Garcia-Granados was harshly critical of Britain's emergency regulations in Palestine, which enabled the High Commissioner to to suspend basic personal rights and liberties at his discretion. Consequently he was rather sympathetic with the underground Irgun movement, whose terrorist activity he considered as political and not criminal in nature. Having failed to induce UNSCOP to hear the testimony of underground leaders, he went (accompanied by Fabregat) to meet them personally. The UNSCOP chairman himself had already seen the Irgun leaders, but kept it secret even from his colleagues.

When the British authorities picked UNSCOP's stay in Jerusalem as the right time to sentence to death three Irgun members who had participated in the attack on the Acre prisons, Garcia-Granados almost exploded, and this time his anti-British indignation carried more weight with his colleagues. He demanded that UNSCOP present Britain with a petition to cancel the sentence, but although he did not have his way most of his colleagues were indignant enough for UNSCOP to issue a statement expressing concern as to the possible repercussions which the executions would have on the Committee's work (June 1947).

Garcia-Granados's militant dissidence was not confined to his anti-British attitude, nor did it end with the termination of UNSCOP's stay in Palestine.

Having arrived at Geneva in late July 1947, UNSCOP began debating the merits of a visit to the Displaced Persons camps in Germany. The Moslem members of UNSCOP (the representatives of India and Iran) were squarely opposed to such a visit on the implied ground that it had nothing to do with the problem of Palestine. Garcia-Granados was vehement in arguing for the visit, and finally it was decided to send the alternates to the camps. Garcia-Granados, Uruguay's Fabregat and the Australian delegate, however, went in person.

In the final phase of his work on UNSCOP, Garcia-Granados

went along with the majority on recommending partition, although he would have liked to avoid partitioning Palestine had he been able to devise any other workable solution.

When, on May 15, 1948, the General Assembly was startled by the news of U.S. instant recognition of Israel, Garcia-Granados was rather annoyed that it was not Guatemala which was the first to recognize the Jewish state. He immediately announced to the Assembly his Government's decision to recognize Israel, although— as he tells it—he had not cleared that announcement with his Foreign Minister due to a faulty telephone connection.

4) To his daughter Alliluyeva's protest that the younger generation of Jews cared nothing for Zionism, he answered, "No! You don't understand. The entire older generation is contaminated with Zionism, and now they're teaching the young people too." Svetlana Alliluyeva, *Twenty Letters to a Friend*, New York, Harper and Row, 1967, p. 196.

5) During the following months when UNSCOP was discussing its report, the question of illegal immigration again became entangled in international diplomacy. The Massad, the Zionist organization that arranged for these migrant ships, were arranging for two more to depart from Rumania. When, as is told in the text, the Soviet representative on October 14 declared Soviet support for partition, the British Foreign Office alleged that Russia was transporting Communist conspiratiors to Palestine.

In summary, over the years the Mossad sent, or attempted to send, about 150,000 illegal immigrants through the British blockade; they came on 96 ships, 18 before the war, 13 during the war, and 65 from 1945 to the end of the Mandate. Bracha Habas, *Gate Breakers*, p. 389.

6) Elizabeth Monroe in her study, "Mr. Bevin's 'Arab Policy,'" page 34, states that the British announcement on September 26, 1947, that it would give up the Mandate took British military headquarters in the Suez Canal zone by surprise, that overnight it had to reverse the movement of troops and military supplies.

7) The suggested UN Commission was to have three to five members, to be chosen by the Assembly and be responsible to the Security Council.

8) He estimated that Britain had spent about 100 million pounds between January 1945 and December 1947 to retain its place in Palestine. House of Commons Debates, January 20, 1948.

9) Harry S. Truman, *Memoirs*, Vol. II, *Years of Trial and Hope*, New York, Doubleday, 1955–56, p. 158.

10) Former Secretary of State Sumner Welles in his book, *We Need Not Fail*, Boston, Houghton Mifflin Co., 1948, p. 63, went so far as to allege that, "By direct order of the White House every form of pressure, direct or indirect, was brought to bear by American officials on the countries outside of the Moslem world who were known to be uncertain or opposed to partition."

11) Shortly afterward the Jewish Agency for Palestine entered into a deal with the Czechoslovak Government to bring many rifles and machine guns, and Gromyko (then in New York for the UN General Assembly) secured Moscow's approval, and during the civil war in Palestine which occurred after the Mandate ended, Czechoslovakia was an important arsenal for the Jewish Army.

12) David Horowitz, *State in the Making*, New York, A. A. Knopf, 1953. Horowitz was a member of the Jewish Agency group then in New York.

13) In the Jewish settlements of Palestine, shouts of joy and sobs mingled with the prayers of thanks. I have a reminiscent memo written by an Israeli who was then a boy living in Haifa that merits a place in the story.

> I remember the day, November 30, when the news arrived. It was a Sunday and I, a boy of eight, was returning home from a trip to the country on the Sabbath recess. Due to some traffic jam I was late to school and, being an exemplary pupil, namely afraid of authority, I had my father accompany me to school to explain to irate authority my unpardonable breach of regulation. When we arrived at school, I cowering with apprehension, our eyes were greeted, instead of the forbidding severity of class-time, with a sight of sheer bedlam. Principal, teachers and students were all outside the school-building, dancing, singing, shouting at the top of their voices. And this, mind you, at 8:30 in the morning (8:00 being the official opening of school-day).
> For me it was a sense of indescribable relief and exhilaration, feeling the restrictions of oppressing authority crumbling in that very

moment, sensing the transition from one state of existence to another, anticipating the creation of a new, completely different,
order of things. This is hardly the record of facts and of grim
reality, but it is the memory of a mood, and I expect that this is
how I shall always remember November 30, 1947.

IV But How Could Partition Be Effected?

1) Elizabeth Monroe, "Mr. Bevin's 'Arab Policy.'"

2) Indicative of the anxieties expressed is the note which Admiral
Leahy wrote in his Diary on January 19, 1948. He was afraid that
the situation would develop into a worldwide war between Moslems
and Christians, or lead to Soviet occupation of the Middle East
and the expulsion of Americans and British from the "oil-rich lands
of the Arabs." Thus, he wrote, the situation was most dangerous
from a military point of view. Leahy was being criticized at the
time by a group which included Einstein and those he characterized
as "well-known pink college professors"; and he told the President
that he regarded these attacks as a high compliment.

3) Truman, *Years of Trial and Hope*, p. 160.

4) In this volume (II) of his *Memoirs* Truman does not tell. In
one paragraph (page 163) he explains that "My policy with regard
to Palestine was not a commitment to any set of dates or circumstances; it was dedication to the twin ideal of international obliga-
tions and the relieving of human misery. In this sense, the State
Department's trusteeship proposal was not contrary to my policy."

5) Jacobson, in 1952, wrote a long letter to Dr. Josef Cohn of the
Industrial Institute of Israel, in which he described vivdly and in
detail this talk with the President, and his subsequent communi-
cations with Weizmann and the President. This is printed in the
American-Jewish Archives for April 1968.
   President Truman's account of this talk in *Years of Trial and
Hope*, pp. 161–162, is brief and uninformative.

6) *Years of Trial and Hope*, p. 190.

7) Jacobson letter, p. 9.

8) *Years of Trial and Hope,* p. 163.

9) Ibid., p. 162.

10) Jacobson letter, p. 10.

11) *Years of Trial and Hope,* p. 162.

V   War and Birth

1) If difference in time is taken into account, about seven hours after.

2) *Years of Trial and Hope,* p. 164.

3) Henderson talk with the author, June 28, 1967, in Washington, D.C.

4) Richard Crossman, *A Nation Reborn,* New York, Atheneum, 1960, p. 82.

5) *New York Times,* September 21, 1948. As Bernadotte's proposals had evolved by September 1948, they contemplated excluding the Negev from Israel and according it the province of Galilee instead (by then captured by the Jews), the internationalization of all of Jerusalem, and turning Lydda and Haifa, both also by then in Jewish hands, into free ports, and requiring Israel to permit all Arab refugees to return to their homes in Israel territory.

6) See for example *New Times* (an official English language publication of the Soviet Government), July 14, 1948, and Gromyko's speech in the Security Council on July 14, 1948.

7) For a description of the tragic assassination, see Aage Lundstrom's *"Epilogue"* in Folke Bernadotte, *To Jerusalem,* London, Hodder, 1951. New York, British Book Centre, 1952.

8) Arthur Koestler, *Promise and Fulfillment, Palestine 1917–1949,* London, Macmillan, 1949.
   Ralph Bunche, the chief UN official in Palestine, was distraught by both the tragic fate of his esteemed colleague and the harm done to the UN authority.

All three candidates for the Presidency of the United States denounced the shocking and vicious atrocity. But in doing so, Henry Wallace, predictably, said that Bernadotte was the "victim of power politics and of British imperialism . . . of the procrastination and duplicity of the mighty powers." *The New York Times,* September 18, 1948.

9) Fighters for Freedom (generally called the Stern Gang). The heads of the group, of course, denied responsibility for the murder.

10) *The New York Times,* October 29, 1948.

11) Israel first applied for membership on November 29, 1948. The measure failed passage in the Security Council. Israel's renewed application passed the Council in April 1949. The matter was then referred to an Ad Hoc Political Committee, which recommended Israel's admission. The General Assembly discussed Israel's application and voted in favor of admission in May 1949.

Index

Abdullah, King, 28
Acheson, Dean, 29
Africa, 23; *see also* North Africa; East Africa
Allenby, General Edmund Henry H., 13
Anglo-American Committee of Inquiry, American and British reaction to recommendations of, 27–31
  conclusions and recommendations of, 26–27
  formation of, 23–24
  personnel of, investigate Palestine question, 25–26
Arabs, 12, 14, 16, 17, 18, 20, 21, 22, 23, 26, 27, 29, 31, 32, 34, 36, 39, 40, 44, 48, 49, 50, 54, 57, 59, 65, 66, 69, 70
  announce they will not abide by U.N. resolution, 46
  armed by British government, 62
  armies of, move on Palestinian Jews, 63–64
  fail to form independent state in Palestine, 68
  oppose U.N. solution to Palestine question, 41
  reaction to U.S. recognition of State of Israel, 62
  relationship with Great Britain, 28
  seek national independence for Palestine, 29
  supply arms to complotters in Palestine, 52
  threaten war if partition in Palestine effected, 45
  U.S. fears war against, 51

Attlee, Clement, 18, 30, 34, 50, 64
  attacks Zionist terrorist activities, 28
  meets with Truman on Jewish question, 24
  proposes formation of Anglo-American Committee of Inquiry, 23
  removes British support of Zionist cause, 21
Austin, Warren, 37, 52, 53, 55, 56, 59
Australia, 37
Austria, 14, 26, 27
Axis, 14
Azerbaijan, 30

Balfour, Arthur James, 12–13
Balfour Declaration, 12–13, 15
Balkan Peninsula, 14
Beeley, Harold, 21
Ben Gurion, David, 60
Bernadotte, Count Folke, 64
  murdered by Jewish terrorists, 65–66
  plans of, to settle war in Palestine, 65, 66
Bevin, Ernest, 18, 21, 24, 28, 30, 31, 34–35, 36, 41, 48, 57, 64
Brussels, treaty of, 54
Byrnes, James F., 25, 35

Cadogan, Sir Alexander, 37, 43
Canada, 37, 42
Chamberlain, Neville, 14
Churchill, Winston, 17, 20–21, 24
Clay, General Lucius, 52
Clifford, Clark, 60, 61
Connelly, Matt, 54
Creech-Jones, Arthur, 41, 58–59

88 Index

Herbert Feis has had a distinguished career as a scholar, as a writer, and as an influential adviser to the U.S. Government. Among his many works are *The Road to Pearl Harbor, Churchill-Roosevelt-Stalin, The Atomic Bomb and the End of World War II, 1933: Characters in Crisis,* and, most recently, *Contest Over Japan. The Birth of Israel* was written in the course of a comprehensive study of relations between the West and the Soviet Union that Mr. Feis is currently completing.